MALMEDY MASSACRE INVESTIGATION

The following report was presented to the Committee on Armed Services by the subcommittee chairman, Senator Raymond E. Baldwin, at the committee meeting on October 13. The report was unanimously approved by the committee and Senator Baldwin thereupon presented it to the Senate on October 14, 1949.

SCOPE OF INVESTIGATION

On March 29, 1949, a subcommittee of the Senate Armed Services Committee, consisting of Senators Raymond E. Baldwin (chairman) Estes Kefauver, and Lester C. Hunt, was appointed to consider Senate Resolution 42. This resolution was introduced for the purpose of securing consideration of certain charges which had been made concerning the conduct of the prosecution in the Malmedy atrocity case and to effectuate a thorough study of the court procedures and post-trial reviews of the case. It must be clearly understood that the function of this subcommittee is a legislative one only. It is not the function of this subcommittee, therefore, to retry the cases, to act as a board of appeals or reviewing authority, or to make any recommendations concerning the sentences. The subcommittee has, however, found it necessary to fully review the investigative and trial procedure in order to make its recommendations.

The investigation automatically divided itself into specific phases; the first dealing with the charges of physical mistreatment and duress on the part of the War Crimes Investigation personnel, and the second covering those matters of law and legal procedure which should be examined in an effort to determine their propriety and the degree to which they might be improved to meet future requirements. As the investigation proceeded, a third phase evolved which has caused considerable concern and which deals with the motivation behind the current efforts to discredit American military government in general, and using the war crimes procedures in particular, as a part of that plan.

During the conduct of the investigations, the subcommittee and its staff held hearings extending over a period of several months, examined 108 witnesses, and independently, as well as through other agencies of the Government, conducted careful investigations into certain of the matters germane to the subject. It should be pointed out that witnesses representing every phase of this problem were heard, including persons who were imprisoned at Schwäbisch Hall and their attorneys, members of the investigating team, members of the court who tried the cases, the reviewing officers who reviewed the record of trial, religious leaders, and other interested parties. Every witness who was suggested to the subcommittee, or whom it discovered through its own efforts, was heard and carefully examined by the members of the subcommittee, other interested Senators, and the subcommittee staff. All affidavits submitted to the committee have been translated and studied. It is felt that the record is complete and adequate to support the findings and conclusions in this respect.

An important part of the investigation was the conducting of a complete physical examination of many of those persons who claimed physical mistreatment, some of whom alleged they received permanent injuries of a nature capable of accurate determination. These examinations were conducted by a staff of outstanding doctors and dentists from the Public Health Service of the United States.

Advice and assistance were also requested from the American Bar Association and other groups with particular knowledge in the field of law and military courts and commissions.

WHAT WERE THE MALMEDY ATROCITIES?

In the minds of a great many persons, the Malmedy atrocities are limited to those connected with the Malmedy crossroads incident which, in fact, is only a part of the charges preferred against the German SS troopers in this particular case. The atrocities with which the accused in the Malmedy case were charged were part of a series committed at several localities in Belgium, starting on December 16, 1944, and lasting until approximately January 13, 1945.[1] They occurred during the so-called Battle of the Bulge and were committed by the organization known as Combat Group Peiper, which was essentially the first SS Panzer Regiment commanded by Col. Joachim Peiper. All the members of this combat team, and particularly those involved in the Malmedy trial were members of the Waffen SS organization.[2] The regiment had had a long and notorious military record on both the western and eastern fronts. On the eastern front, one of the battalions of the Combat Group Peiper, while commanded by Peiper, earned the nickname of Blow Torch Battalion after burning two villages and killing all the inhabitants thereof. Peiper had at one time been an adjutant to Heinrich Himmler.[3] The prisoners under investigation were for the most part hardened veterans.

Basically, the atrocities which were committed at 12 places throughout Belgium consisted, according to accounts of different witnesses, of the killing of approximately 350 unarmed American prisoners of war, after they had surrendered, and 100 Belgian civilians. It was one of the few cases where substantial numbers of Americans were murdered en masse. The location and approximate number of persons murdered at these various points are contained in the following table:[4]

	Prisoners of war	Civilians
Honsfeld, Dec. 17, 1944	19	
Bullingen, Dec. 17, 1944	50	1
Crossroads, Dec. 17, 1944	86	
Ligneuville, Dec. 17, 1944	58	
Stavelot, Dec. 18–21, 1944	8	93
Cheneux, Dec. 17–18, 1944	31	
La Gleize, Dec. 18, 1944	45	
Stoumont, Dec. 19, 1944	44	1
Wanne, Dec. 20–21, 1944		5
Lutrebois, Dec. 31, 1944		1
Trois Ponts Dec. 18–20, 1944	11	10
Petit Thier, Jan. 10–13, 1945	1	

[1] Charge sheet appendix, subcommittee hearings, p. 1572.
[2] Record of trial, pp. 32 to 70.
[3] Record of trial, cross-examination Peiper, pp. 1288, 1289, 1968.
[4] Compilation of figures contained in review by deputy judge advocate for war crimes.

DEVELOPMENT OF PRETRIAL INVESTIGATION

Concurrently with the defeat of the Germans in the so-called Battle of the Bulge, investigations were started concerning the massacre of American prisoners of war. This preliminary work resulted in a determination that the Malmedy massacre had in all probability been perpetrated by personnel of the Combat Team Peiper, who were scattered throughout prison camps, hospitals, and labor detachments in Germany, Austria, the liberated countries, and even the United States.[5] Conditions in the prison camps, however, were such that after interrogation, those interrogated were able to rejoin their comrades and all soon knew exactly what information the investigators desired.[6] It became clear that the suspects could not be properly interrogated until facilities were available which would prevent them from communicating with each other before and during and after interrogation. According to the evidence submitted to the subcommittee, it was during this period that it became known that prior to the beginning of the Ardennes offensive, the SS troops were sworn to secrecy regarding any orders they had received concerning the killing of prisoners of war.[7] In accordance with the plan for further investigation of this case, all the members of the Combat Team Peiper were transferred to the internment camp at Zuffenhausen. They were initially there housed in a single barracks where it was still impossible to maintain any security of communication between the accused.[8] During this time it was learned that Colonel Peiper gave instructions to blame the Malmedy massacre on a Major Poetchke, who had been killed in Austria during the last days of the war.[9] These orders were carefully followed by those under investigation. Accordingly, further steps were deemed to be necessary, and those prisoners who were still suspect were evacuated to an interrogation center at Schwabisch Hall, where they were housed in an up-to-date German prison, but where during investigation they were kept in cells by themselves.[10] Initially there were over 400 of these prisoners evacuated to Schwabisch Hall, and from time to time others were transferred to the prison, up to and including the latter part of March 1946. It was during this period of interrogation at Schwabisch Hall that the alleged mistreatment of prisoners took place.

FINDINGS AND CONCLUSIONS

For the purposes of this report, the matters under discussion are separated according to the three phases of the investigation set out above, i. e.: (1) Matters of duress during the pretrial investigation; (2) trial and review procedures; and (3) the manner in which current situation has been agitated.

1. Matters of duress during pretrial investigation

During 1948 and 1949 charges were made which caused considerable publicity concerning the treatment of these SS prisoners at Schwabisch Hall. The prisoners were confined at Schwabisch Hall from December 1945 to April 1946 and the pretrial investigations occurred then.

---

[5] Subcommittee hearings, pp. 34, 270; record of trial, Ex. p. 27.
[6] Subcommittee hearings, pp. 34, 271.
[7] Subcommittee hearings, p. 34.
[8] Subcommittee hearings, pp. 34, 271.
[9] Subcommittee hearings, p. 34.
[10] Subcommittee hearings, pp. 34, 272, 1241, 1242.

In April 1946 the pretrial investigations having been completed the prisoners were removed to Dachau.[11] There their trial began on May 16 and continued until July 16.

Shortly after the defense counsel began to work on the case at Dachau, they prepared a questionnaire for distribution to the accused, which contained, among other things, questions concerning any physical abuses or duress.[12] The subcommittee made every effort to secure the original of these executed questionnaires but they were apparently destroyed when the case was over. As a result of information furnished on these questionnaires and statements that had been made concerning duress, the defense counsel before trial, through their chief counsel, Col. Willis M. Everett reported the matter to the Third Army judge advocate in charge of war crimes.[13] Colonel Everett later conferred with the deputy theater judge advocate general for war crimes who ordered an investigation to be conducted at once by Lt. Col. Edwin J. Carpenter, who testified before the subcommittee.[14] During his investigation which was completed before the trial, between 20 and 30 of the accused who made the most serious charges of duress were examined.[15] According to Colonel Carpenter's testimony before the subcommittee, which was confirmed by independent testimony given by the interpreter used by him at that time, only four of this group stated that anyone had abused them physically.[16] These four did not claim physical abuse in connection with securing confessions, but rather punchings and pushings by guards while being moved from one cell to another.[17] However, during his investigation, considerable emphasis was placed on the use of so-called mock trials, solitary confinement, and mention was made of the use of hoods, and insults.[18] The investigating officer in this case (Colonel Carpenter), and the deputy theater judge advocate for war crimes (Col. Claude B. Mickelwaite), to whom these charges were made stated to the subcommittee that they felt the seriousness of the matters reported by the defense counsel were not established and therefore were not of particular import, but that the use of some of the tricks, and in particular the mock trials had been established, and should be explained to the court at the start of the trial so that it could weigh evidence introduced in the light of the accusations made by the accused.[19]

At the time of the trial 9 of the 74 accused took the stand in their own behalf. Of this number, 3 alleged physical mistreatment. The court was thereby placed on notice of the charges of physical mistreatment made by those who took the stand in their own behalf, and apparently did not feel that it was of such importance as to require any further investigation or study.[20] Some 16 months after conviction practically every one of the accused began to submit affidavits repudiating their former confessions and alleging aggravated duress of all types.[21] (The word "confession" has been used to de-

[11] Subcommittee hearings, p. 407.
[12] Subcommittee hearings, pp. 36, 576, 885.
[13] Subcommittee hearings, pp. 428, 920, 1560, 1561.
[14] Subcommittee hearings, pp. 428, 884, 920, 1564.
[15] Subcommittee hearings, pp. 887, 942, and Everett.
[16] Subcommittee hearings, pp. 887, 942.
[17] Subcommittee hearings, pp. 893, 942–943.
[18] Subcommittee hearings, pp. 887, 889, 942–943.
[19] Subcommittee hearings, pp. 891, 920.
[20] Subcommittee hearings, pp. 1393, 1423.
[21] Subcommittee files.

scribe the documents secured from the prisoners. These were in fact, in large part, statements which described places, dates, and events in which the signer took part or witnessed the acts and conduct of other accused.) These affidavits were secured by German attorneys, particularly Dr. Eugen Leer, a defense counsel at the trial, who is the most active attorney in this case at the present time.[22] These affidavits were later used by Col. W. M. Everett in his petition to the Supreme Court for a writ of habeus corpus in this case.[23] In addition, affidavits to such matters were, in a few cases, submitted by others who were at Schwabisch Hall but who were not defendants in the case.[24] Many of these affidavits were so lurid in their claims as to shock even the most calloused reader. The subcommittee accordingly has gone to great lengths to attempt to establish the facts as they pertain to these matters.

Before proceeding with an item-by-item discussion of the types of duress alleged by various persons, it is necessary to describe in some detail the prison at Schwabisch Hall and its method of operation. The prison is located in the heart of a thriving and prosperous city of approximately 25,000 population and is a modern stone-and-concrete prison for civil prisoners. Since it is located at the foot of a hill, it is possible for persons living next to the prison, on the higher ground, to look down into the prison yard, and on quiet nights to hear sounds from within the prison enclosure.

The prison was taken over by the United States authorities primarily for use as an internment center for political prisoners. However, when it was decided to concentrate the Malmedy suspects at this point, a portion of the prison was set aside for the housing and interrogation of these men.[25] They were separated completely from the political prisoners, with the exception of a few of the internees who performed routine prison duties. These few gained some knowledge of the handling of the Malmedy suspects, but were forbidden to speak to them.[26]

The administration of Schwabisch Hall prison was under the control of the Seventh Army and there was a detachment stationed at the prison for this purpose. This group was headed by a Capt. John T. Evans, who testified before the subcommittee and who described in detail the normal prison administration. His organization was responsible for the housing, guarding, feeding, clothing, medical care, well-being, and all other matters pertaining to the prisoners.[27] The men who conducted the interrogation were members of a war crime investigating team sent down to the prison from the War Crimes Branch through Third Army Headquarters. They had no responsibility other than to prepare the case for trial and no control over the administrative functions of the prison.[28]

There was a considerable difference in the method in which the Malmedy suspects and the political prisoners were handled. The medical care of the Malmedy prisoners was charged to an American medical detachment stationed at the prison, with necessary hospitali-

[22] Subcommittee hearings, p. 1433.
[23] Subcommittee hearings, exhibit A, p. 1189.
[24] Subcommittee files, exhibit 23—accused affidavits attached to petitions filed by Dr. Eugen Leer on February 1, 1948, April 12, 1948, June 16, 1948, and August 24, 1948.
[25] Subcommittee hearings, pp. 34, 272, 323, 805, 1241.
[26] Subcommittee hearings, pp. 116, 643, 864, 1256.
[27] Subcommittee hearings, p. 323 et seq.
[28] Subcommittee hearings, pp. 35, 273, 346, 911, 1059, 1242, 1243.

zation being handled in nearby United States Army hospitals. According to the testimony given the subcommittee, all such medical matters were handled by American medical personnel, and only a few of the dental cases were treated by a German civilian dentist, who came into the prison periodically for the purpose of treating the internees. As to the manner of providing dental care, there is considerable variance in the testimony introduced before the subcommittee, and it will be discussed in detail later in this report. The internees were cared for by German medical personnel who were interned in the prison or who were brought in from the outside.[29]

The interrogation team, consisting of approximately 12 members,[30] set up offices in one wing of the prison. They were primarily on the second floor, and in this same wing there were cells used for interrogation as well as for the administrative activities of the team.[31] In addition there were five cells which in design and construction were different from the normal cells found throughout the prison.[32] The subcommittee checked many of the prison cells. The normal ones, without exception, were well-lighted, adequate in size for two or more occupants, had toilets,[33] and were on a central heating plant with radiators that apparently were working during the time the prison was occupied by the Malmedy suspects.[34] These cells were of solid construction with a solid door containing a small peephole through which the occupant could be seen and heard. Loud conversation or noise within the cells could be heard by occupants of other cells, and, of course, if they called through the windows it could be heard pretty generally throughout the prison.[35] The five cells referred to, which were located immediately adjacent to the cells used for interrogation, differed in that they had smaller windows which were higher in the room and therefore did not give as much light. The cells were adequate, as far as size was concerned, for one or two occupants.[36] They all had flush toilets. However, there was an interior iron grille immediately inside the main door which separated the prisoner from the door itself.[36] Food could be, and according to testimony before the subcommittee was, passed to the prisoners through an aperture in the steel grille at the lower part of the grille on the right-hand side as the cells were entered.[36] It was in these five cells that prisoners were retained during certain phases of their interrogation. They have been labeled by various persons as death cells, dark cells, and solitary confinement cells. From the standpoint of physical confinement, there is no evidence before the subcommittee to indicate that these cells were any worse than are to be found in any normal prison. However, there is much conflicting testimony as to their use. Members of the interrogation team, testifying before the subcommittee, stated that no one was confined in these cells for longer than 2 or 3 days at a time, during which they received normal treatment and rations.[37] Other statements have been made to the effect that prisoners were kept in the special cells for weeks on end,[38] and,

[29] Subcommittee hearings, pp. 129, 326, 334, 335, 641, 845, 847, 848, 862, 864 et seq., 1256.
[30] Subcommittee hearings, p. 31.
[31] Visual examination by subcommittee; subcommittee hearings, pp. 34, 273, 340, 822, 1262.
[32] Visual examination by subcommittee; subcommittee hearings, p. 335.
[33] Visual examination by subcommittee; subcommittee hearings, pp. 128, 328, 336, 865.
[34] Visual examination by subcommittee; subcommittee hearings, pp. 324, 351.
[35] Visual examination and tests by subcommittee; subcommittee hearings, p. 335.
[36] Visual examination and tests by subcommittee.
[37] Subcommittee hearings, pp. 36, 49, 118, 1241, 1242.
[38] Subcommittee files, Leer petitions and affidavits.

some alleged, without food.[39] Others said they were fed but stayed there for long periods.[40] In that connection it should be pointed out that there are only five such cells and several hundred suspects were screened during a period of 4 months.[41]

The bulk of the Malmedy suspects were housed in a cell block in a wing of the prison which was separated from the interrogation cells by a courtyard.[42] Immediately adjacent to this wing, in which most of the Malmedy prisoners were housed, was a separate building which contained, on the second floor, a hospital dispensary used mainly for the political internees.[43] The ground floor contained the prison kitchen. Up until the time individuals under interrogation for the Malmedy crimes had completed their interrogation, they were moved through this courtyard and between other points, with a black hood over their heads in order to insure security insofar as their knowing who else was under interrogation.[44]

1. Mock trials

The subcommittee found that, in not more than 12 cases of the several hundred suspects interrogated by the war crimes investigation team, mock trials were used in an effort to elicit confessions and to soften the suspects up for further interrogation. The evidence given concerning these trials is extremely conflicting, even among the persons who alleged they were subject to a mock trial. There is no question that mock trials were used.[45] The members of the prosecution staff stated that the results obtained were very unsatisfactory and that they used this procedure, which they called the schnell procedure, on only the less intelligent and more impressionable suspects.[46]

The subcommittee believes the general facts about the trials to be undisputed. There was a table within a room, which was covered with a black cloth and on which was a crucifix and two lighted candles. Behind this table would be placed two or three members of the war crimes investigation team, who, in the minds of the suspects, would be viewed as judges of the court. A prisoner would be brought in with his hood on, which was removed after he entered the room. Two members of the prosecution team, usually German-speaking members, would then begin to harangue the prisoner, one approaching the matter as though he were the prosecutor or hostile interrogator, and the other from the angle of a defense attorney or friendly interrogator.[47] The subcommittee could find no evidence to support the position that the suspect was told, specifically in so many words, that anyone was his defense attorney. However, there is no question that the suspect quite logically believed that one of these persons was on his side, and may have assumed that he was his defense counsel.[48] The subcommittee does not believe that these mock trials were ever carried through to where a sentence was pronounced, nor was any evidence found of any physical brutality in connection with the mock trials

[39] Subcommittee files, Leer petitions and affidavits.
[40] Subcommittee files, Leer petitions and affidavits.
[41] Subcommittee files, pp. 34, 35, 136, 272.
[42] Visual inspection by subcommittee; subcommittee hearings, p. 366.
[43] Visual inspection by subcommittee; subcommittee hearings, pp. 647, 648, 1261.
[44] Subcommittee hearings, pp. 35, 346, 353, 367, 1276, 1300, 1326.
[45] Subcommittee hearings, pp. 41 et al., 134 et al., 276, 352 et al., 666, 1267, 1299, 1330.
[46] Subcommittee hearings, pp. 134, 806.
[47] Subcommittee hearings, pp. 40, 117, 118, 157, 162, 276, 340, 397, 723, 807, 831, 872, 1267, 1268.
[48] Subcommittee files, posttrial affidavits of accused.

themselves. In fact, one witness who was attacking the war crimes investigation team procedures testified that there was no brutality in connection with a mock trial at which he had served as a reporter.[49] When these mock trials had reached a certain point they would be disbanded and the prisoner taken back to his cell, after which the person who had posed as his friend would attempt to persuade the suspect to give a statement.[50]

The subcommittee feels that the use of the mock trials was a grave mistake. The fact that they were used has been exploited to such a degree by various persons that American authorities have unquestionably leaned over backward in reviewing any cases affected by mock trials. As a result, it appears many sentences have been commuted that otherwise might not have been changed.[51] It is interesting to note why such a procedure was started. Lieutenant Perl, one of the interrogaters, stated that the so-called mock trials were his suggestion, and had been patterned after German criminal procedure with which the suspects were familiar.[52] Since he was a native-born Austrian, and a continental lawyer, the procedures seemed proper to him.[53] Because of the great attention paid to the mock trials by the Simpson Commission, and because Judge Van Roden publicized them so thoroughly, the subcommittee has made a comprehensive study of the pretrial procedure prevalent on the Continent. The full report on this subject is a part of the subcommittee records.[54]

It is a fact that in France, Germany, and Austria there is an established pretrial examination procedure in which an examining judge hears evidence from any and all persons concerned. Generally speaking, this procedure is only used in the most important criminal cases. During this pretrial investigation the evidence that is secured may be of the most circumstantial nature, but it is later admissible at the real trial for such probative value as the court desires to place upon it.[55] The subcommittee is fully of the opinion that this was the basis for the use of the so-called mock trials, even though they differed in the window dressing and stage effects that the interrogation team used for their own purposes.

2. Solitary confinement

The subcommittee feels that there is no doubt that many of the suspects in the Malmedy case were kept in separate cells for extended periods of time, but has no criticism or complaint of this normal practice. This is because it was necessary to keep the suspects separated until interrogation was completed. The preponderance of evidence showed beyond a reasonable doubt that such confinement was under the most favorable conditions that the circumstances permitted, and that during this time the men were fed, were warm, and suffered no more inconvenience than one would normally except to find in an ordinary civilian prison in the United States.

3. Short rations and bread and water

The subcommittee is convinced that, with the exception of one occasion, the suspects in the Malmedy matter were fed three ade-

[49] Subcommittee hearings, p. 157 et seq.
[50] Subcommittee hearings, p. 276.
[51] Subcommittee hearings, exhibit Y.
[52] Subcommittee hearings, pp. 722, 724 et seq.
[53] Subcommittee hearings, p. 724 et seq.
[54] Subcommittee hearings, exhibit S.
[55] Subcommittee hearings, exhibit S.

quate meals a day. Some of the persons who had been interrogated at Schwabisch Hall testified before the subcommittee, and on other occasions, that the food supply was adequate,[56] which corroborates completely the statements of the administrative staff of the prison, including the American medical personnel, who were categoric in stating that the prisoners were well fed.[57] The one exception was in late December 1945, during a period of time which varies according to the testimony from four meals, according to the American medical personnel, to 4 days, according to some of the suspects in the case, during which all of the Malmedy suspects were placed on bread and water.[58] It is an established fact that it was punishment placed on the group because of the efforts of some of the prisoners to communicate with others by marking the bottoms of their mess kits.[59] It was also testified that it required some time to eradicate the markings from these utensils before they were put in use again.[60] The American medical officer in charge stated that when he learned that they were on a bread and water diet, he went to the prison commander and the chief of the war crimes investigation team and told them that he would not permit bread and water punishment to be given unless properly reported. Accordingly it was stopped.[61] The subcommittee was unable to ascertain accurately as to how many regular meals the prisoners missed. Varying testimony ranged from four meals to 4 days.[62] However, the prisoners received adequate bread and water during this period which punishment is both legal and sometimes used within our own Navy and Marine·Corps. Other than this, there appears to be no evidence that the prisoners were either starved or placed on short rations, and certainly it should not have affected the securing of evidence by the war crimes investigating team.

4. Failure to supply drinking water

A quite frequent allegation made by the suspects was that they received no drinking water during the entire period of their incarceration, and were forced to drink from the toilets in their cells.[63] The subcommittee does not feel that there is any foundation for this charge, or competent evidence to support it. This conclusion is arrived at first because of the direct testimony to the contrary by members of the American administrative staff, including the guards, the doctors, medical personnel, and the members of the war crimes investigating team.[64] This evidence taken by itself might not be conclusive, but several of the suspects who were interrogated by the subcommittee testified that they received regular food, a change of underwear once a week, shaving equipment and washing water every morning, but no drinking water.[65] On cross-examination those who alleged they received no water gave conflicting answers, and admitted they received other liquids with their meals.[66] One, who claimed he never received

[56] Subcommittee hearings, pp. 1473 et seq., 1503.
[57] Subcommittee hearings, pp. 323, 351, 821, 846, 864.
[58] Subcommittee hearings, pp. 298, 827, 846.
[59] Subcommittee hearings, pp. 186, 298, 827, 846.
[60] Subcommittee hearings, pp. 298, 827.
[61] Subcommittee hearings, pp. 846, 847.
[62] Subcommittee hearings, pp 186, 187, 298, 847, 1473.
[63] Subcommittee files, affidavits of accused; subcommittee hearings, p. 1479.
[64] Subcommittee hearings, pp. 128, 328, 644, 821, 865.
[65] Subcommittee hearings, pp. 1478, 1479.
[66] Subcommittee hearings, p. 1498.

drinking water during his entire stay at Schwabisch Hall, had previously testified he had been on bread and water for 4 days.[67] There was competent testimony that one of the duties of the guards was to bring water when called for by the prisoners, and not one was denied water when he asked for it. The subcommittee does not feel that such charges can be supported, because it is difficult to believe that a group of people who were admittedly supplying all of the necessities of life to the suspects would deliberately deprive them of drinking water.

5. Use of hoods

It is an undisputed fact that hoods were placed over the heads of the suspects when they were moved from their various cells and back and forth around the prison.[68] Some few isolated charges have been made that the hoods were bloody and dirty.[69] The subcommittee accepts without question the fact that the hoods were used, but in view of the previous difficulties incurred in this case when no security was used, and the necessity of keeping from one prisoner the knowledge of other suspects who also were being questioned, the subcommittee does not condemn the use of the hoods. Members of the prison administrative staff, testifying before our subcommittee, stated that they personally had inspected the hoods; that they were not dirty, and they had never seen any evidence of blood on any of the hoods.[70] However, the subcommittee recognizes that it would be possible for hoods used for such purposes to become dirty, or, in the event of an accident, or through deliberate action of an individual, for them to have become bloody, without the responsible persons knowing of it. However, the weight of evidence shows to the contrary, and the subcommittee feels that the particular charge of hoods being bloody is unproven.

6. Beatings, kickings, torture, and other physical brutality

Many of the accused in the Malmedy trial, as well as the so-called eye witnesses, have testified that they were beaten severely and sadistically, not only by guards moving them around the prison, but by the staff of the war crimes investigating team, for the purpose of securing confessions.[71] By constant repetition, and the multiplicity of these charges, they have been accepted by some persons as fact. They have been published repeatedly in various forms. In attempting to arrive at the facts in this case, the subcommittee first of all studied the affidavits prepared by the accused some 16 months after conviction, in which the accused claimed beatings, torture, and other duress, for the purpose of securing confessions. The subcommittee noted that an investigation was made of these charges before the trial, when the defense attorneys alleged duress to the war crimes authorities, and an investigation was ordered.[72] Evidence was introduced before the subcommittee to show that only four of those alleging duress at that time claimed to have been beaten, and that those claimed the beatings had been administered by guards and not for the purpose of obtaining confessions.[73] The subcommittee further noted that shortly thereafter when the accused were being tried, nine of the accused took

---

[67] Subcommittee hearings, p. 1498.
[68] Subcommittee hearings, pp. 35, 123, 367, 806, 831, 1039.
[69] Subcommittee files, affidavits of accused; subcommittee hearings, p. 161.
[70] Subcommittee hearings, p. 646.
[71] Subcommittee files, affidavits of accused, of German witnesses.
[72] Subcommittee hearings, pp. 883 et seq., 920.
[73] Subcommittee hearings, pp. 887, 943.

the stand in their own behalf, and of these nine, three alleged physical beatings or mistreatment.[74] The allegations do not appear to have impressed the court at that time. The subcommittee took note of the testimony submitted to it by the defense counsel and in particular the testimony of Lt. Col. John S. Dwinnell, the associate chief defense counsel, who stated that he had been primarily responsible for the decision that no more of the accused should take the stand in their own behalf. He stated that this decision was made because those who did testify were lying to save themselves to such an extent that they were prejudicing the cases of other defendants.[75]

The subcommittee also took note of the fact that one of the witnesses for the prosecution, Kurt Kramm, was the subject of a highly disputed ruling by the court when the court refused to permit the defense attorneys to cross-examine Kramm as to whether or not his testimony had been secured as a result of duress.[76] The subcommittee studied with great interest the ruling of the court and found that the ruling appeared to be technically correct, for the matter had not been raised on direct examination. No foundation had been laid for the fact that the defense counsel in asking the question was attempting to attack the credibility of the witness or his testimony when the ruling was made. The subcommittee noted that the defense attorneys did not contest the ruling and stated that it was expected that Kramm would return to the stand. There is no question that he could have been called as a defense witness. However, the defense did not call Kramm to testify regarding any physical duress used on him. The subcommittee took notice of the many statements made by defense attorneys, church people, and others concerning brutality but found that, without exception, they were hearsay to the witnesses and were predicated primarily on the affidavits submitted by the accused themselves after conviction.[77] The subcommittee took particular note of first-hand evidence given by persons who were in Schwabisch Hall at the time these brutalities were alleged to have occurred.[78] Dr. Edouard Knorr, a civilian dentist who treated internee prisoners at the prison, made an affidavit to the German defense attorneys stating that he had treated 15 to 20 [79] of the Malmedy prisoners for injuries to the mouth in which teeth had been knocked out and in one case had treated a man for a ruptured jaw.[80] Dr. Knorr died this year of arteriosclerosis and so was not available as a witness. The subcommittee, through investigation, discovered the whereabouts of his assistant who had accompanied him on most of his trips to Schwabisch Hall, and summoned her as a witness. This assistant made an impressive witness before the subcommittee and endeavored to corroborate the statements made in Dr. Knorr's affidavit.[81] She testified that she had seen very few of these things with her own eyes, but that Dr. Knorr told her of them.[82] Furthermore, Dr. Knorr had been approached by German defense attorneys for his affidavit, and she had helped him to prepare it.[83] She also had been approached by attorneys after the death of Dr. Knorr for the purpose

[74] Record of trial, pp. 2354, 2415, 2439.
[75] Subcommittee hearings, p. 438 et al.
[76] Record of trial; subcommittee hearings, p. 422.
[77] Subcommittee hearings, pp. 170, 594, 1561.
[78] Subcommittee hearings, pp. 1469 et seq., 1499 et seq., 1513 et seq., 1523 et seq., 1528 et seq.
[79] Subcommittee hearings, p. 604; subcommittee files.
[80] Subcommittee files, Knorr affidavit.
[81] Subcommittee hearings, p. 1523 et seq.
[82] Subcommittee hearings, p. 1524.
[83] Subcommittee hearings, p. 1525.

of securing her own affidavit, and she had discussed it before preparation with the defense attorneys.[84]   She was asked if Dr. Knorr had maintained any dental records of the Malmedy patients treated by him.   She stated that records had been kept but that they had been destroyed some time ago on Dr. Knorr's orders.   She testified further that normally they maintained records of everyone treated by Dr. Knorr for 10 years, but that these particular records had been destroyed within a couple of years after the patients were treated.[85]   Certain aspects of the dental testimony are discussed later in the case in connection with the thorough medical examination made by the doctors.

An internee prisoner by the name of Dietrich Schnell prepared an affidavit on October 1, 1948, at the request of Mrs. Sepp Dietrich, the wife of General Dietrich, one of the accused in this case.[86]   This affidavit indicated a meticulous and exact knowledge of everything that went on in Schwabisch Hall at the time the Malmedy prisoners were there.[87]   If the statements were true, they would raise a strong presumption that all the charges made in the various accusations were correct.

Dietrich Schnell is an extremely intelligent former Nazi paratrooper. Before the war he was a kreisleiter in the Nazi Party in the vicinity of Goppingen.[88]   A kreisleiter was one of the bulwarks of the Nazi Party, and within his area, which consisted of approximately 50,000 persons, Schnell literally had life-and-death authority over the people. Schnell was located by the staff of the subcommittee and interrogated at some length.   A copy of that interrogation, which is contained in the subcommittee's record, indicates clearly that he had carefully memorized the most minute details of his affidavit, including details of conversations which had been held some 3 years earlier.[89]   He later was examined under oath by the subcommittee.[90]   On direct questioning, which went beyond the material in the original affidavit, he changed his story in substantial detail.   The conflict in evidence was very noticeable because of the contrast with the exactness of his knowledge of all the matters in his original affidavit.   The subcommittee took particular notice of the statements made in his affidavit concerning the suicide of one of the suspects named Freimuth.   In his affidavit he gave considerable details of the Freimuth matter, including the words he used when he was alleged to have shouted from the window of his cell to Schnell.[91]   When the prison was physically examined by the staff of the subcommittee, with Schnell along for the purpose of checking the various parts of his story, it was noted that the cell number given in his affidavit, and which was confirmed by other evidence, was an interior cell from which Freimuth could not have been seen by Schnell.   This fact standing by itself casts doubt on the authenticity of Schnell's affidavit.   When he later appeared before the subcommittee, he had grasped the significance of the situation and attempted to change the location of the cell and its number by verbal testimony.[92]

[84] Subcommittee hearings, p. 1527.
[85] Subcommittee hearings, p. 1524, 1525.
[86] Subcommittee files, p. 1528, subcommittee files, affidavits.
[87] Subcommittee files, Schnell affidavit.
[88] Subcommittee hearings, p. 1543.
[89] Subcommittee hearings, exhibit V.
[90] Subcommittee hearings. p. 1528 et seq.
[91] Subcommittee files, Schnell affidavit.
[92] Subcommittee hearings, p. 1541 et seq.

His entire story indicated that it had been carefully prepared and rehearsed. Reduced to its essential detail and under examination, the only direct testimony that he gave to any beating by members of the war crimes interrogation team was one instance which he claimed to have seen quite late at night from a window in the dispensary. He stated, on interrogation, that he saw Lieutenant Perl strike and then kick an accused being questioned.[93] The room in which he claimed he saw this done was established to be the administrative office used by the war crimes investigating team.[94] It was denied by witnesses that this room was ever used for interrogation.[95] Further, they testified that there was interrogation at night on only one occasion.[96] That one interrogation was not conducted by Perl. When Schnell first gave this story on interrogation, he described meticulously how Perl had struck the prisoner with the back of his hand and then demonstrated the way he then kicked him.[97] However, Schnell was taken to the prison and placed at the window in the dispensary where he could look into the room in which the alleged incidents were supposed to have taken place. By test it was determined that even a tall man could not be seen below the waist and that it would have been impossible for anyone to have seen a man kick another and describe it as Schnell had done on the preceding evening.[98] He then qualified his earlier statement that he saw Perl kick the man and said he had merely seen a movement of his body which indicated that he was kicking a man, after which the suspect staggered back into the room.[99] Schnell also alleged that he had seen the guards beat prisoners with clubs as they were being moved from point to point around the prison.[1] This particular charge was made by others who submitted affidavits but was denied by other witnesses.[2] Schnell also volunteered the information that a set of gallows had been in the courtyard. Later examination of German guards, who had been present at the time the Malmedy prisoners were there, disclosed that no gallows had ever been in Schwabisch Hall.[3] When confronted with their statement, Schnell qualified his statement by saying that the gallows had not been erected but had been on the ground and covered with canvas.[4] This was at complete variance with his earlier story.[5] One other very significant item in connection with Schnell's approach to this case transpired after interrogation by the subcommittee staff. He stated definitely that he had not been in touch with any German attorneys or lawyers in this case but had prepared his affidavit at the request of Mrs. Sepp Dietrich.[6] Through investigation the staff discovered that immediately after interrogation he called Dr. Eugen Leer, a German attorney, who has apparently been coordinating the activities of all these prisoners.[7]

The subcommittee is convinced the Schnell, because of his Nazi affiliations, was a most interested witness. Because of the many

[93] Subcommittee hearings, p. 1593.
[94] Subcommittee hearings, p. 1262.
[95] Subcommittee hearings, p. 1263.
[96] Subcommittee hearings, pp. 1131, 1261.
[97] Subcommittee hearings, pp. 1590, 1537.
[98] Visual inspection by subcommittee.
[99] Subcommittee hearings, p. 1538.
[1] Subcommittee hearings, p. 1529.
[2] Subcommittee files, affidavits of accused.
[3] Subcommittee hearings, staff report (Chambers).
[4] Subcommittee hearings, p. 1535.
[5] Subcommittee hearings, pp. 1535, 1595.
[6] Subcommittee hearings, p. 1590.
[7] Subcommittee hearings, staff report.

discrepancies in relatively minor matters and because of the definite and substantial error in connection with the Freimuth suicide, the subcommittee feels it should give little credence to the testimony of Schnell. Moreover, it is clear that it was intended to fit into the pattern of well-prepared, well-organized testimony, aimed at substantiating the various allegations made concerning brutality.

Another witness by the name of Otto Eble was located through the counterintelligence forces in Europe in the French zone. Eble was the man who alleged that he had had burning matches placed under his fingernails and was the only one, as far as the subcommittee could discover, who alleged that "phony" priests had been used in securing confessions.[8] On examination, the subcommittee developed the fact that Eble, who had signed his affidavit as "Otto," was in fact named Friedrich Eble; that he had taken his brother's name of Otto and his rank and used them during the period of time he was under investigation.[9] Furthermore, he has a record of four convictions on the charge of embezzlement, and on occasion, while an internee, escaped and lived for many weeks until discovered under the name of Erwina Sennhausen, an alleged Swiss citizen.[10] On interrogation by French intelligence officers, his brother Otto, whose name had been used, stated that the truth was not in his brother Friedrich.[11] While testifying before the subcommittee, he gave three separate and distinct stories as to why he used his brother's name and rank, and each of them was probably untrue. A physical examination was made of Eble to determine if there were any scars indicating burns under his fingernails, which he stated had become infected. No evidence was found to support his claim. The doctors who examined him stated that in their opinion the man was a pathological liar and was incapable of telling the truth.[12]

The obviously false charges made by this man Eble have been thoroughly publicized by Judge Edward L. Van Roden and others.[13] They have spread as truth the false statements of this convicted criminal and liar, not only throughout our country but abroad.[14] The results of such publicity have been so serious abroad as to warrant the special attention of the subcommittee. Furthermore, the subcommittee cannot but comment that those citizens of the United States who have accepted and published these allegations as truth, without attempting to secure verification of the facts, have done their country a great disservice.

In summary, the subcommittee considered the following evidence on the subject of physical brutality and mistreatment after translating and studying all the affidavits and statements submitted to it. First of all, it accepted as evidence the affidavits submitted by the Germans accused after conviction.[15] It is recognized that these affidavits were self-seeking, and under examination most of them have not been corroborated by the medical evidence and other subcommittee investigations. Second, the subcommittee heard the testimony of persons who claimed to be eyewitnesses at Schwabisch Hall of these

[8] Subcommittee files, Eble affidavit attached to Leer petition dated April 12, 1948.
[9] Subcommittee hearings, p. 1516.
[10] Subcommittee hearings, pp. 1519, 1520, 1521.
[11] Subcommittee files and hearing p. 1599.
[12] Subcommittee hearings, p. 1628.
[13] Subcommittee files, article from the Progressive, news release of National Council for Prevention of War.
[14] Subcommittee files, material furnished by Dr. Leer, Dr. Aschenauer, and confidential material.
[15] Subcommittee files, affidavits submitted by Dr. Leer et al.

various matters, and their testimonay has been analyzed in some detail earlier in the report.[16]   Third, the subcommittee heard the arguments made by defense attorneys, both American [17] and German,[18] which were not evidence in the normal sense but expressed conclusions on the part of witnesses.   Fourth, there were several witnesses, namely Bailey,[19] Tiel,[20] and Sloane,[21] who testified before the subcommittee, who in their testimony indicated that they had seen incidents which would appear to corroborate, in kind, the statements alleged by the convicted accused.   On the other hand, the subcommittee heard the testimony of Lt. Col. Edwin J. Carpenter [22] and his interpreter, Paul G. Guth,[23] who made an investigation of these alleged physical mistreatments prior to the trial, and whose findings did not support to the slightest degree the claims of physical brutality made in later affidavits by the convicted accused.   The subcommittee also heard testimony from the war crimes interrogation team personnel,[24] which admittedly was from interested witnesses, but whose testimony was given forcefully and convincingly.   Many of these individuals had requested to testify so that they could state their position under oath before the subcommittee.   These individuals all testified, categorically, that none of these physical mistreatments or brutalities occurred.

The subcommittee also heard members of the administrative staff of the prison,[25] who were responsible for the care and guarding of the prisoners.   These witnesses had no self-interest in this matter, and testified strongly and definitely to the fact that there was no physical mistreatment of the prisoner.   This testimony was particularly convincing, since it included the testimony of the doctors and medical enlisted personnel who were assigned to Schwabisch Hall for the purpose of caring for the suspects in this case.   The subcommittee itself secured a medical staff, consisting of two doctors and a dentist of outstanding qualifications, from the Public Health Service of the United States.   This medical staff independently examined all the Malmedy prisoners who are presently at Landsberg Prison.[26]   In addition, they also examined Eble [27] for evidence of physical abuse. They state, of those convicted prisoners at Landsberg, 11 claim that they were not physically mistreated at Schwabisch Hall, 34 allege they were physically mistreated at Schwabisch Hall but do not claim to have received injuries which would leave evidence of a permanent nature, and 13 allege that they were physically mistreated and have injuries of a permanent nature.[28]   The medical staff pointed out that there was no question that the 11 prisoners were not subjected to physical mistreatment at Schwabisch Hall and that the second group of 34 prisoners had no physical evidence to support their claims of alleged physical mistreatment.[29]   Of the 13 who alleged physical mistreatment with permanent results, the medical evidence does not

[16] Subcommittee hearings, pp. 1513, 1523, 1528 et seq.
[17] Subcommittee hearings, see index.
[18] Subcommittee hearings, see index.
[19] Subcommittee hearings, p. 154 et seq.
[20] Subcommittee hearings, p. 543 et seq.
[21] Subcommittee hearings, p. 897 et seq.
[22] Subcommittee hearings, p. 883 et seq.
[23] Subcommittee hearings, p. 939 et seq.
[24] Subcommittee hearings, see index.
[25] Subcommittee hearings, see index.
[26] Subcommittee hearings, p. 1616 et seq.; also committee files.
[27] Subcommittee hearings, p. 1624 et seq.
[28] Subcommittee hearings, pp. 1618, 1624.
[29] Subcommittee hearings, pp. 1618, 1624.

support, to any degree, the claim of these prisoners.[30] They state that 3 had conditions which definitely were not due to physical mistreatment, and that the remaining 10 showed physical findings which might possibly have resulted from physical mistreatment, but none of these 10 showed evidence of the severe acts alleged by the prisoners.[31]

All of the facts and evidence brought to the attention of the subcommittee through the above sources were analyzed and weighed carefully, and the subcommittee believes there is little or no evidence to support a conclusion that there was physical mistreatment by members of the interrogation team in connection with their securing evidence in the Malmedy case. The preponderance of evidence is all to the contrary and there are too many discrepancies which appear in the allegations made concerning such physical mistreatment. On the other hand, the subcommittee recognizes that in individual and isolated cases there may have been instances where individuals were slapped, shoved around, or possibly struck, but is convinced that if this did occur it was the irresponsible act of an individual in the heat of anger in a particular situation. Furthermore, it definitely was not a general or condoned practice. There is no substantial evidence to support the belief that any persons were affected, insofar as their convictions were concerned, by physical mistreatment of this kind, even if it might have occurred in isolated cases. The subcommittee is convinced that the confessions made by the prisoners, and the evidence submitted at the trial were not secured through physical mistreatment of the accused.

7. *Posturing as priests*

The charge that members of the American interrogation team postured as priests for the purpose of securing confessions has been widespread throughout our country. This is primarily due to the speeches made by Judge Edward L. Van Roden and the publication of his remarks by the National Council for the Prevention of War, and other similar organizations.[32] The sole source of the charge was, insofar as the subcommittee was able to determine, the witness Eble [33] whose testimony was discussed in detail above. For the reasons previously stated, the subcommittee believes that absolutely no credence can be given to any statement made by Eble, who is a convicted criminal and a liar, and that there is no truth to this charge. It is considered most unfortunate that many prominent religious people have been misled by the use of the uncorroborated statements of this man, and apparently accept the allegation as being true. As will be noted throughout this report, many of the most flagrant charges which have been so widely publicized in this case can be attributed first to the affidavit prepared by Eble, second to the cloak of authority given to his statement through the media of the publications and speeches of Judge Van Roden, and third by the organized dissemination of this information both in our country and abroad by the National Council for the Prevention of War.

8. *Inadequate medical facilities*

Many of the affidavits submitted by the persons interrogated at Schwabisch Hall alleged that they were denied medical attention for

---

[30] Subcommittee hearings, pp. 1618, 1624.
[31] Subcommittee hearings, pp. 1618, 1624.
[32] Subcommittee files, Progressive article and news articles.
[33] Subcommittee files; affidavit of Eble attached to Dr. Leer's petition dated April 12, 1949.

such ailments as they might have.[34]   There is no question that there was an American doctor and enlisted personnel stationed at Schwabisch Hall at all times while the Malmedy prisoners were there.[35] These doctors testified before the subcommittee,[36] as did their superior, Captain Evans.[37] Their testimony was clear, professional, and convincing. It is clear that they had complete responsibility for the physical condition of the suspects and that they made every effort to meet their responsibilities.   It was also noted that while some suspects allege they did not receive medical attention, many other affidavits make reference to treatment by medical officers, enlisted personnel, and trips to American medical facilities away from Schwabisch Hall.[38] These latter statements made by some of the suspects corroborate the statements made by the American personnel.   Therefore, it is the opinion of the subcommittee that there were adequate medical facilities available and in use for the Malmedy prisoners at Schwabisch Hall. In this connection, the affidavit of Dr. Knorr should again be examined.[39] In this affidavit he claimed that he had treated 15 to 20 cases in which teeth had been knocked out and in 1 case a ruptured jaw. The dental member of the subcommittee's staff examined the teeth of all the accused who were convicted and who were confined at Landsberg Prison. He examined several cases in which teeth were alleged to have been knocked out. His report is contained in the subcommittee record and throws considerable doubt on the truth of the allegations.[40]   It should be noted that only one of this group claimed to have been treated by a German civilian dentist. The rest all stated they were treated by American dental personnel at various points.[41] This tends to place doubt on the accuracy of the affidavit of Dr. Knorr.

9. Threats against families of the accused, and fraternization with wives of the accused

Several of the affidavits in this case allege that members of the interrogation team threatened the prisoners by telling them that ration cards would be taken away from their families and other punitive measures would be taken against them if the suspects in question did not confess.[42]   The degree to which such threats were used is hard to establish, but the subcommittee believes that in some cases some of the interrogators did make threats of this kind.   It is questionable as to the effect such statements would have on the type of individual under interrogation, but it is hard to believe that this by itself would make a man perjure himself to the point of making a false confession and bearing false witness against his comrades.   Therefore, the subcommittee concludes that in some cases such threats might have been used but believes they were not general in character.

There were no charges made that members of the interrogation team fraternized with wives of the accused prior to the time of trial.   How-

---

[34] Subcommittee files, affidavits of accused attached to petitions prepared by Dr. Leer dated February 2, April 12, June 16, and August 24, 1948.
[35] Subcommittee hearings, pp. 355, 640, 844, 862.
[36] Subcommittee hearings, pp. 844, 862.
[37] Subcommittee hearings, p. 322 et seq.
[38] Subcommittee files, affidavits of accused submitted by Dr. Leer.
[39] Subcommittee files, affidavit attached to Dr. Leer's petition of June 16, 1948.
[40] Subcommittee hearings, p. 1616 et seq.
[41] Subcommittee hearings, p. 1616 et seq.; subcommittee files.
[42] Subcommittee files, accused's affidavit attached to Dr. Leer's petition.

ever, it was developed by the Raymond Board [43] that subsequent to the trial, but before sentences were passed, two members of the interrogation team took several of the wives to the officers club where it was obvious that they were drinking together.   While this could have had no possible effect on the outcome of the trial, in the opinion of the subcommittee it showed a lack of good judgment on the part of the individuals concerned and should not be condoned.   One of those involved, who was not an interrogator, but a clerk with the interrogation team, was sent back to the States as a result of this incident, and the other, testifying before the subcommittee stated that it was the only time that such a thing had occurred, and that he had been wrong.[44]   His attitude was such as to convince the subcommittee that all realized that a mistake had been made.   There were no charges or evidence that any other members of the investigating team ever fraternized with the wives of the accused.   The subcommittee assumes it is the sole incident and that it has been properly handled by the responsible authorities.

10. Use of stool pigeons

Many of the affidavits alleged that the interrogation team used stool pigeons for the purpose of securing evidence.[45]   This is freely admitted by the members of the interrogation team as a part of their normal practice,[46] and the subcommittee finds no grounds for complaint for such activities.   Traditionally the use of stool pigeons has been practiced by our American prosecuting authorities and is a recognized practice in criminal investigations.

11. Tricks of various kinds and mental duress

Practically all of the affidavits alleged that the prisoners had been tricked or mentally harassed to a point where they became confused and as a result signed false confessions.[47]   The subcommittee made a determined effort to find the nature of these various tricks. Apparently the members of the interrogation team gave considerable thought as to how they could break down the resistance, silence, and deception on the part of an individual in order to get him to talk.   The pretended use of microphones; [48] the pretense of having information from other accused implicating the suspect being interrogated; [49] the plus and minus system, whereby members of the interrogation team would keep a score in front of the man, putting down a plus when he told the truth and a minus when he was thought to be lying, thereby leading him to believe that mathematically they were going to determine his guilt by the answers he gave; [50] the indentification of a particular mark on his body; [51] and the confronting of individuals with other members of the organization who had turned state's evidence.[52]   All of these methods were used for the purpose of getting the prisoners to talk. There is no question that such methods were used.   The subcommittee feels that they cannot condemn them since they represent the usual and accepted methods used in criminal investigations.   It would seem

[43] Subcommittee files, report of Administration of Justice Review Board, EUCOM, testimony of Harry Thon. Subcommittee hearings, p. 1281.
[44] Subcommittee hearings, pp. 1281, 1283.
[45] Subcommittee files, accused's affidavits attached to Dr. Leer's petition.
[46] Subcommittee hearings, pp. 278, 807.
[47] Subcommittee files, accused's affidavits attached to Dr. Leer's petition.
[48] Subcommittee hearings, pp. 662, 827.
[49] Subcommittee hearings, pp. 224, 614, 628, 805, 806.
[50] Subcommittee hearings, p. 1269.
[51] Subcommittee hearings, p. 524.
[52] Subcommittee hearings, pp. 661, 696, 803.

that the bulk of the success of this interrogation stemmed from the ability to confuse and deceive a group of persons who had had an opportunity to prepare their stories in advance, and who to a marked degree were involved in a conspiracy to avoid the consequences of the acts in which they had participated. These prisoners with a few exceptions were hardened, experienced members of the SS who had been through many campaigns and were used to worse procedure.

12. *Promises of acquittal*

It was charged that many of the statements were obtained through promising a man that he would go free if he told the truth and thereby implicated others.[53] Considerable argument and discussion has already been had on this particular point, and the evidence submitted to the subcommittee is very conflicting. There is no question but that the interrogation team published instructions in the form of SOP No. 4, which in section 4 discussed this particular matter.[54] There is no question but that section 4a specifically forbids that any promise of acquittal be made, but 4b appears to be a modification of the prohibition in the earlier section. All the members of the interrogation team who testified before the subcommittee stated that no one was promised that he would not be tried if he would turn state's evidence and implicate others.[55] In fact, SOP No. 4 required that before anyone could make such a promise the officer in charge of the interrogation team had to approve such an agreement, and they categorically stated that this was not done. Therefore, it is the belief of the subcommittee that while SOP No. 4 would appear to indicate that such arrangements could have been made, it does not appear from the evidence before the subcommittee that any such promises were made. It is recognized that it is quite a common practice in criminal cases for state's attorneys in the United States to get a man to turn state's evidence upon the promise that if he tells the truth he would be recommended to the court for leniency. Here again, the subcommittee finds it extremely difficult to assess blame because of the instructions issued by the interrogation team, particularly since it appears that these instructions were never put into operation. However, this is an area in which great care must always be exercised and there is no question that SOP No. 4 was ambiguous in its phraseology. The subcommittee believes that the final decision as to whether or not any immunity should be granted should be the decision of the court and not of those responsible for conducting the interrogation of suspects.

13. *Fake hangings*

Several of the persons who submitted affidavits in this case testified that they were either threatened with hanging or in fact did have a rope placed around their necks and were pulled up off their feet several times until they lost consciousness.[56] One of those who made this claim was Eble,[57] whose testimony has been thoroughly discredited and is completely unacceptable to this subcommittee. Many witnesses were questioned as to whether any of them ever saw ropes or a rope being used in Schwabisch Hall. This has been denied by every-

---

[53] Subcommittee files, accuseds' affidavits attached to Dr. Leer's petition.
[54] Subcommittee hearings, p. 272, see exhibit, p. 1229.
[55] Subcommittee hearings, pp. 503 et al., 663, 824, 825, 1278.
[56] Subcommittee files, affidavits of accused attached to Dr. Leer's petition.
[57] Subcommittee files, Eble's affidavit attached to Dr. Leer's petition of April 12, 1948, subcommittee hearings, p. 1515.

one [58] with the exception of a witness who testified that prisoners were led around with a rope about their necks.[59]   All witnesses questioned on this point, with the exception of Eble,[60] denied that such practices were ever followed.   The subcommittee feels in the absence of competent evidence to support the allegations concerning hangings that, in fact, they never happened.

II

MATTERS PERTAINING TO THE TRIAL AND REVIEW PROCEDURES

(Supplemental report to be rendered when American Bar Association reports)

The rules of procedure under which this case was tried were not those that are used by the Anglo-Saxon nations in regularly constituted military or civilian courts.[61]   In attempting to evaluate the manner in which the court was conducted, the subcommittee soon found that it was impossible to do so until this point was clearly understood.   For this reason, a brief history of the development of the war crimes procedures should be of interest.

In 1945, the London conference drew up a charter for international military tribunals [62] to implement the decision to treat as war criminals individuals of the separate states who violated the so-called rules of war.   The prosecution of war criminals is nothing new in the history of our country.   After practically all of our wars, our own military courts have tried members of the enemy forces who were charged with the commission of war crimes.[63]   However, this war brought into being for the first time the concept of an international military court for the trial of war criminals.

Prior to the late war there was an unwritten international doctrine that heads of states would not be held responsible for acts committed by them in such capacity.   The decision of the London conference which resulted in the London agreement, and the charter of the International Military Tribunal before which Goering and other major Nazi leaders were tried and convicted, represented the views and decisions of the major Allied Powers engaged in that war.   Personal responsibility of heads of states and of individuals for offenses committed by them was recognized and set down as accepted principles of the laws of war.[64]   The International Military Tribunal for the Far East adopted these principles in the trials of the major Japanese war criminals. Both of these tribunals were composed of the representatives of several of the nations involved in the conflict in each area.

The rules of procedure adopted for the trials before the international military tribunals represented a compromise between the various legal procedures of the several Allied nations.   They were a composite of Anglo-Saxon and continental codes of justice.

The subsequent proceedings against other major Nazi war criminals at Nuremberg were conducted before military tribunals authorized by the Allied Control Council for Germany (Control Council Law No. 10). They were appointed by the zone commander, United States zone,

[58] Subcommittee hearings, pp. 346, 367 et al.
[59] Subcommittee hearings, p. 158.
[60] Subcommittee hearings, p. 1515.
[61] Military Government Manual for Legal Officers, p. 11, par. 14; also Military Government Regulations, title 5, sec. 593 (a); subcommittee hearings, p. 922 et seq.
[62] Subcommittee hearings, pp. 918, 1583.
[63] Subcommittee hearings, p. 918 et seq.
[64] Subcommittee hearings, p. 1584.

Germany, and were composed of American personnel, who for the most part were judges from various State courts of the United States. The rules under which these courts operated were the same as those under which the first Nuremberg tribunal operated,[65] and such courts have been regarded as international in character.

In addition, the various nations, within their respective zones of occupation in Germany,[66] and in other areas, established their own national military courts for the trial of lesser war criminals charged with violations of the laws of war. In the American zone these courts were called military government courts which under appropriate directives were created especially for the trial of war criminals. It appears that in general the rules of procedure under which these courts operated were an adaptation of the rules of procedure adopted for the Nuremberg trial. The court that tried the Malmedy case was of this type.

The Malmedy trials deal with violations of laws and customs of war long recognized as such; specifically, the murder of prisoners of war and noncombatant civilians. The Geneva (prisoner of war) convention of July 27, 1929, and the Annex to Hague Convention No. IV of October 18, 1907, sets out a positive duty to protect prisoners of war against acts of violence and prohibits the killing or wounding of an enemy who had laid down his arms and no longer has a means of defending himself.

In connection with procedure it is pertinent to quote from the Technical Manual for Legal Officers prepared by SHAEF. This was the basis for later rules of procedure which governed American military government courts. Section 14 of that manual reads as follows:

MILITARY LAW.—The law of military government thus created should not be confused with the statutory law of the respective United Nations governing their armed forces.

Further, this manual also contains a guide to procedure in military government courts, and in paragraph 9, section 1, the following quote brings out one of the basic differences between the system employed in this case, and that normally followed by our civilian or military courts:

9. EVIDENCE.—Rule 12 does not incorporate the rules of evidence of British or American courts, or of courts martial. The only positive rules binding upon the military government courts are found in rule 12 (3), rule 17, and rule 10 (5). Hearsay evidence, including the statement of a witness not produced, is thus admissible, but if the matter is important and controverted, every effort should be made to obtain the presence of the witness, and an adjournment may be ordered for that purpose. The guiding principle is to admit only evidence that will aid in determining the truth.

The military government court at Dachau, which tried the Malmedy case, was operating under these rules of procedure.

Composition of the court

The accused in the Malmedy case were tried before a general military government court appointed by paragraph 24, Special Orders No. 90, Headquarters, Third United States Army, dated April 9, 1945, which was subsequently corrected by paragraph 32 of Special Orders No. 117, Headquarters, Third Army, dated May 10, 1946.[67]

---

[65] Subcommittee hearings, p. 918.
[66] Subcommittee hearings, p. 918.
[67] Subcommittee hearings, p. 1574.

The following officers were members of the court:
1. Brig. Gen. Josiah T. Dalbey.
2. Col. Paul H. Weiland.
3. Col. Lucien S. Berry.
4. Col. James G. Watkins.
5. Col. Wilfred H. Stewart.
6. Col. Raymond C. Conder.
7. Col. A. H. Rosenfeld, law member.
8. Col. Robert R. Raymond, Jr.*

Time and facilities available to the defense

One of the complaints made by the defense counsel was that they were not given adequate time to prepare their case for defense.[68] They pointed out that there were 74 accused in this case, and that the pretrial interrogation was completed about the middle of April, and on April 17 or 18 the accused were brought to Dachau where the trial was to be held. The trial began on May 16.

Col. Willis M. Everett, Jr., chief defense counsel, was appointed in the early part of April, but it was not until April 11 that the defense counsel were able to start assembling.[69] When finally organized about April 20 the defense staff consisted of Col. Willis M. Everett, Jr., Lt. Col. John S. Dwinnell, Lt. Col. Granger G. Sutton, Capt. B. N. Narvid, Second Lt. Wilbert J. Wahler, Mr. Herbert J. Strong, Mr. Frank Walters; and the following German counsel: Drs. Max Rau, Heinrich M. Wieland, Otto Leiling, Franz J. Pfister, Eugen Leer, and Hans Hertkow.[70] Of this group, the experience and capabilities of the defense counsel varied to a considerable degree, but Colonel Everett, Colonel Dwinnell, and, it was reported, Lieutenant Wahler had had considerable court experience. The German attorneys were lawyers of considerable experience but were not familiar with the manner in which American military courts functioned.[71]

Testimony before the subcommittee shows that the initial group meeting was about April 20, and that all the time prior to that was considered by the defense counsel to be lost time, excepting that Colonel Everett, the chief defense counsel, and two others, were making administrative arrangements such as securing table, desks, telephones, etc.[72] This physical equipment was requisitioned from the Army, and there was no particular difficuty in getting delivery of all the necessary items.[73] Testimony also indicated that it was not until approximately 2 weeks before the trial started that the defense counsel received the bulk of the pretrial statements made by the accused, and what was purported to be the bills of particulars on which the individuals and the entire group would be tried.[74]

The record discloses that there was a maximum of approximately 4 weeks for the defense to get ready before the trial started, which appears to be too short a time for the study and development of a proper defense, in a case of such major proportions, and in which there were 74 accused. It was further testified before the subcommittee that it was a very difficult proposition to secure the confidence

---

*Excused by verbal orders of commanding general and did not participate in any of the proceedings.
[68] Subcommittee hearings, pp. 408 et seq., 605, 1557.
[69] Subcommittee hearings, p. 415.
[70] Subcommittee hearings, p. 406; record of trial, p. 314.
[71] Subcommittee hearings, pp. 406, 1557.
[72] Subcommittee hearings, p. 415.
[73] Subcommittee hearings, pp. 405, 415.
[74] Subcommittee hearings, p. 412.

of the accused, and of course there were language differences which made the defense problem more difficult.[75]

It is recognized that the defense did have some opportunity to continue with their preparations for the presentation of their case during the time that the prosecution was presenting its case, and that there was a recess of approximately 7 days, after the prosecution rested its case before the defense had to commence. There is no record that the defense requested further time for the purpose of preparing their case. It is assumed that if such a request had been made and properly supported, it would have been granted. There is evidence that Colonel Everett discussed the matter with higher authorities, and that an administrative decision had been made that there would be no adjournment,[76] but there is no record anywhere that a request was made to the court, which, in the final analysis would be the group which should grant such a motion for postponement.[77]

Notwithstanding these facts, the subcommittee is of the opinion that due to the limited time available, the defense was considerably handicapped in preparing its case for trial. The subcommittee does not believe that this seriously affected the outcome of the trial. In the future courts should assure themselves that a reasonably sufficient time has been allowed for this purpose.

Insofar as facilities are concerned, the preponderance of the evidence before the subcommittee indicates that the Army supplied everything that the defense needed, as rapidly as possible, and assisted them in this respect to the greatest possible extent.

Trial of the accused en mass

One of the complaints made by the defense counsel in this matter was that the court did not allow a severance of the various defendants in this case. A motion of severance was filed with the court which was denied.[78] The granting of such a motion was, of course, within the discretion of the court, and the subcommittee does not feel that it has the authority to serve as an appellate court to judge the ruling in this particular case. The subcommittee feels that it is one of its responsibilities, however, to comment on matters which might be improved in the case of future trials of this kind. It is noted that on a review of this matter by the War Crimes Review Board, it was stated in conclusion that—

It does not appear that the denial of the motion resulted in an injustice to any of the accused to such a degree as would warrant a new trial.

When so many accused, of varying ranks, are being tried together on a single charge, there must be some conflict of interest between the superiors and the subordinates. On the other hand, it is recognized that the scarcity of officers, and the time elements that are involved in matters of this kind, made it extremely difficult to conduct large numbers of trials for separate defendants.

The subcommittee feels that this basic rule should govern cases of this kind. Where there is more than one defendant and it appears that their joint indictment and trial will result in a conflict of interest to the extent that an individual defendant or group of defendants will

[75] Subcommittee hearings, pp. 415 et seq., 1560.
[76] Subcommittee hearings, pp. 413, 1557.
[77] Subcommittee hearings, p. 1557.
[78] Subcommittee hearings, p. 416.

be so seriously prejudiced as to prevent a fair and just trial, they should be indicted and tried separately or appropriate severances granted.

The Kramm case

The defense attorneys, and the various petitions for review in this case, have laid considerable stress on a ruling by the court in connection with the testimony of Kurt Kramm. This man was a prosecution witness.[79] On cross-examination defense counsel attempted to raise the question of duress which had not been raised on direct examination. The law member of the court sustained the objection of the prosecution on the ground it was beyond the scope of the direct examination.

In order that this matter may be completely understood the following quotations are made from the petition to the Supreme Court of the United States, filed by Col. Willis M. Everett in this case:[80]

The witness Kramm testified on cross-examination:
"Q. In what period of time did you take part in that Russian campaign which you first mentioned?
"PROSECUTION. I object.
"Colonel ROSENFELD. Objection sustained. Not cross-examination" (record, p. 215).
Cross-examination of the witness:
"Q. Now, how often would you say you were approximately interrogated at Schwabisch Hall?
"PROSECUTION. I object.
"Colonel ROSENFELD. Objection sustained.
"Mr. STRONG. May I very respectfully point out to the court, with due deference, that this is cross-examination * * *
"Colonel ROSENFELD. It is not cross-examination, because it is without the scope of the direct examination. The court has ruled. The objection is sustained.
"Q. Kramm, isn't it a fact that you, during the time you were in Schwabisch Hall, signed a statement for prosecution, in question-and-answer form, consisting of approximately 20 pages?
"PROSECUTION. I object again.
"Colonel ROSENFELD. That is not cross-examination. It is the last time the court will notify you." (record, p. 216).
"DEFENSE COUNSEL. May it please the court, on behalf of the defense and in view of the fact that the witness will return to the witness stand at a later time during this trial, no further questions will be asked of the witness at this time, but we as defense counsel would like at this time an amplification of the court's ruling on the objection by the prosecution to our line of questions on cross-examination. Do we understand that in the future we will be limited to the line of questioning on direct examination of the witness, or will we be permitted to ask of the witness questions designed primarily to attack the credibility and veracity and bias of the witness?
"Colonel ROSENFELD. Both the prosecution and the defense will be permitted to cross-examine the witness other than the accused according to the rules and regulations of cross-examination. Where the credibility of the witness is to be attacked, the credibility will be attacked in the prescribed manner and the court will permit such attack.
"If the accused or any of the accused take the stand, cross-examination will be permitted in accordance with the rules of evidence whereby the accused may be cross-examined on any matter in connection with the case" (record, p. 220–221).

Testimony given before the subcommittee indicates that the defense counsel made no effort to lay a foundation for the attack on the credibility of the witness or to attack the manner of interrogation at Schwabisch Hall, nor did they notify the court that this was the purpose of this line of questioning.[81] For this reason it appears that the ruling of the court was technically correct.

[79] Record of trial, p. 186.
[80] Subcommittee files.
[81] Subcommittee hearings, pp. 1371, 1373, Rosenfeld; record of trial, Kramm testimony.

Although the subcommittee does not take the position that it has the authority to pass on the propriety of rulings made by the court, it appears that the defense counsel, either through lack of knowledge as to how such an attack should be made on the credibility of the witness, or for other reasons, did not exercise the proper diligence in pressing this point. The subcommittee feels that it is the duty of the law member of the court to make certain that legal technicalities do not prevent the court from hearing all pertinent testimony. Therefore the law member should have advised the defense counsel as to the proper procedure to use in laying a foundation for an attack on the credibility of the witness.

It is noted in the quoted matter above that defense counsel said that they did not desire to cross-examine further at that time because they expected that this witness would again be on the stand, and the inference was that they intended to call him as a defense witness, at which time they could have asked such questions on direct examination as they saw fit. The subcommittee hesitates to draw an inference from the fact that Kramm was not called to the stand by the defense for the purpose of bringing out any matters of duress that might have affected his credibility as a witness for the prosecution.

Failure of witnesses to take the stand in their own behalf

One point which was developed during the course of the subcommittee's investigation, which is believed to be of great importance in this case, is the failure of the defense to permit all the accused to take the stand in their own behalf.[82]

First of all, through testimony introduced before the subcommittee by various persons, including the German defense counsel, and Lieutenant Colonel Dwinnell, it appears that it took considerable persuasion and argument on the part of certain of the American defense counsel to persuade the accused not to take the stand. On the surface, that appears to be most unusual. It is the opinion of the subcommittee that it is an inherent right of an accused to take the stand in his own defense. Normally, defense counsel hesitates to persuade a client as to the properness of his course in such a matter. He usually limits himself to a presentation of the various things that could happen, but leaves the decision strictly up to the defendant. In this case, Colonel Everett and Lieutenant Colonel Dwinnell decided that it was best that the defendants not take the stand in their own behalf, and argued strongly with them until they convinced them that that was the proper course of action.[83]

Until the time of that argument, nine of the defendants had taken the stand in their own behalf.[84] Lieutenant Colonel Dwinnell, in testifying before the subcommittee, stated that these were lying so much that they were "like a bunch of drowning rats. They were turning on each other, and they were scared; and, like drowning men clutching at straws, they would say: 'No; I was not at the Crossroads, I'm certain I was not, but so-and-so was there,' trying to get the ball over into his yard. So we called a halt. Now, how can we properly represent 74 accused that were getting so panicky that they were willingly saying things to perjure themselves?"

[82] Subcommittee hearings, pp. 438, 1564 et seq.
[83] Subcommittee hearings, pp. 439, 1564, 1565 et seq.
[84] Record of trial and subcommittee hearings, p. 442.

Colonel Everett states that he could not support this statement because he did not know whether they were lying or not.[85] He felt that, with the defendants turning on each other, the case of all was being weakened. Further, he believed that the prosecution expected this to happen. These facts led to his decision not to put any more on the stand.

Furthermore, Lieutenant Colonel Dwinnell said that, in his opinion, the prosecution had not established a prima facie case,[86] and that he believed that the court would not convict the defendants.[87] He further stated that they requested an adjournment of 2 hours for the purpose of conferring with the accused to convince them that they ought to quit, and finally they did. Lieutenant Colonel Dwinnell also testified that there was considerable disagreement initially between not only members of the American counsel but between the American and German counsel, and that it took considerable persuasion on his part to convince the group that they should no longer take the stand.[88]

The subcommittee is unable to judge what testimony would have been introduced into the record, and what effect it would have had on the court, had each defendant testified in his own behalf. On the other hand, some 16 months after conviction, many of these accused made claims of physical mistreatment which they said caused them to execute their original confessions or statements.[89] It would seem entirely likely that, had these statements been proven at the time of the trial to the satisfaction of the court and reviewing authorities, they might have served as the basis for a different decision in this case. Therefore, the subcommittee is of the opinion that the defense counsel in this case either did not believe the stories of the defendants, of which they apparently had knowledge, concerning physical mistreatment, or that they erred grievously in not introducing such testimony into the record.

It is difficult for the subcommittee to reconcile the fact that this was not done, and the apparent acceptance and support of the various members of the defense counsel now give to the affidavits submitted some 16 months later by the defendants in this case.

Lack of information furnished defense attorneys

One complaint made before the subcommittee was to the effect that, because of the manner in which decisions are handed down in military courts, there is no detail to support or explain why a particular individual was convicted.[90] Although it was represented to the subcommittee by Dr. Leer that copies of the trial proceedings were not available to defense attorneys, the subcommittee is of the opinion that this was an exaggeration and that copies actually were furnished daily to certain defense counsel. On the other hand, the subcommittee agrees that it is essential that the completed record of trial to be made available to all defense counsel, and this apparently was not done in this case.[91]

Reviews and studies of this case

The subcommittee was keenly interested in the various reviews and investigations that were made by the Army of the Malmedy case, and

[85] Subcommittee hearings, p. 1565.
[86] Subcommittee hearings, p. 438.
[87] Subcommittee hearings, pp. 438, 1564.
[88] Subcommittee hearings, p. 439.
[89] Subcommittee files. See petitions and affidavits supporting it.
[90] Subcommittee hearings, pp. 1345, 1436 et seq.
[91] Subcommittee hearings, p. 1569.

the apparent effort that was made to make certain that no accused suffered because of procedural or pretrial errors.

As in all war-crimes cases, the findings and sentences of the court had to be reviewed by the staff judge advocate.[92] In this case the procedure provided for an initial review by the deputy theater judge advocate for war crimes. Thereafter, there was a review by a war-crimes board of review in the office of the theater judge advocate, which considered the recommendation of the earlier review.[93] Both of these reviews were then considered by the theater judge advocate, who made recommendations to the commanding general of the theater (General Clay), who took final action on the cases.[94]

In this connection, the subcommittee noted that initially the case was assigned for review to an attorney, a civilian employee, by the name of Maximilian Koessler, who testified before the subcommittee.[95] The record shows this attorney had worked on the case for 5 months, and had reached a decision in only 15 of the 73 cases.[96] The decisions he had reached differed in a considerable degree from those finally approved by the commanding general, but in some cases Mr. Koessler's recommendations were more severe than those finally approved.[97]

According to the testimony before our subcommittee, Mr. Koessler went into such detail in his reviews that it unduly delayed the completion of the consideration of the case; and therefore, after 5 months the review of the Malmedy case was reassigned to other lawyers in the office of the deputy theater judge advocate for war crimes.[98] In due time, the initial review was completed, and the case was forwarded to the theater judge advocate for further study and transmission for final approval by the commanding general.

In order to assist the theater judge advocate in his decisions, he had created a second review board known as the war-crimes board of review.[99] This group reviewed the case in detail and made recommendations to the theater judge advocate. They differed in a substantial number of cases with the initial review, and, generally speaking, were considerably more lenient than the deputy judge advocate for war crimes.[1]

The theater judge advocate then took the recommendations of the war-crimes board of review, along with the record of trial, and the initial review, and made his recommendations to the commanding general. Some idea of the results of these various reviews can be gained when it is pointed out that, while there were 43 death sentences adjudged by the court, only 12 were finally approved by General Clay. There were also reductions in sentences in 41 cases, including the original death sentences, and 13 outright disapproval of sentences.[2]

The subcommittee noted one procedure which it believes to be wrong, and which should not be permitted, although in this case the matter reacted to the benefit of the defendants. Lieutenant Colonel Dwinnell, who had been the associate chief counsel for the defense in the Malmedy matters, was assigned to the war-crimes board of review as an adviser to the group that were reviewing the Malmedy

[92] Subcommittee hearings, p. 1575.
[93] Subcommittee hearings, pp. 417, 1061, 1164.
[94] Subcommittee hearings, p. 1163.
[95] Subcommittee hearings, p. 926.
[96] Subcommittee hearings, p. 1362.
[97] Subcommittee hearings, p. 1362.
[98] Subcommittee hearings, p. 926.
[99] Subcommittee hearings, p. 1163.
[1] Subcommittee hearings, p. 588.
[2] Subcommittee hearings, p. 588.

case.[3] This meant that Lieutenant Colonel Dwinnell was in a position to and did influence the recommendations of that review board in favor of the defense.[4] On the witness stand, he stated in response to a question as to whether he argued any of his points before the review board as follows, "Every day for the defense".[5] It is believed to be highly improper that any person who has had any connection with the trials in any capacity whatsoever should be assigned to a position in which he could influence the reviews of these cases. This assignment of Lieutenant Colonel Dwinnell might account for the fact that the war-crimes board of review recommended a great many more disapprovals and a greater degree of leniency than was finally recommended by the theater judge advocate, and approved by the commanding general of the theater.[6]

Subsequent to these various reviews, which, in effect, were three and possibly four up to this point, there have been two studies made by the Army of this case. On July 23, 1948, Secretary Royall created the Simpson Commission, which was composed of Judge Gordon A. Simpson, of Texas, and Judge Edward L. Van Roden, of Pennsylvania.[7] This Commission was assigned the responsibility of making an analysis of all the unexecuted death sentences awarded by the Dachau courts, which were 139 in number. Of these 139 unexecuted death sentences, 12 were Malmedy cases.

The Simpson Commission arrived in Europe on July 30, 1948, and submitted their report on September 14, 1948. Among other recommendations made by them was that the 12 death sentences in the Malmedy case be commuted to life imprisonment.[8] Testimony before our subcommittee adduced the fact that this recommendation was made because they believed that the pretrial investigations in the Malmedy case may not have been properly conducted, and they felt that no death sentence should be executed where such doubts existed.[9]

It is interesting to note that Judge Simpson stated categorically to the subcommittee that in his opinion there had been no physical mistreatment of the accused in the Malmedy matters,[10] but that the use of the mock trials and similar matters had influenced him in his decision.

However, Judge Van Roden, in testifying before our subcommittee, and in speeches and publications after having seen the same evidence and heard the same witnesses as Judge Simpson, violently attacked practically all phases of the pretrial examination. While he admitted in his testimony that he had no direct evidence of physical mistreatment he stated that he was convinced that many of the matters alleged by the accused, after conviction, were fact, and that he had made his recommendations accordingly.[11]

An examination by the subcommittee of the list of witnesses interviewed by the Simpson Commission shows clearly that not a single member of the pretrial investigation team or of the prosecution staff at the trial, were interviewed; nor did these individuals have an op-

[3] Subcommittee hearings, pp. 423, 447, 1165.
[4] Subcommittee hearings, pp. 423, 447.
[5] Subcommittee hearing, p. 447.
[6] Subcommittee hearings, p. 588.
[7] Subcommittee files, Simpson Report.
[8] Subcommittee files, Simpson Report.
[9] Subcommittee hearings, pp. 220, 1088.
[10] Subcommittee hearings, pp. 208, 212.
[11] Subcommittee hearings, pp. 243, 245, 259 et seq., 1068, 1092; article in the Progressive magazine and news stories.

portunity to submit affidavits concerning their activities in the Malmedy matter.[12] It is noted, however, that defense counsel, oth American and German, were heard; religious leaders, and many others who were interested witnesses and who were strongly advancing the theory that the evidence secured by the prosecution in this case had largely been secured through duress were also heard.[13]

Judge Van Roden, on his return to the States, according to the evidence before the subcommittee, made a number of speeches and collabroated in articles in which he stated as fact that the American interrogators tortured, beat, and abused the defendants until their confessions were secured.[14] The statements made by Judge Van Roden were not supported by Judge Simpson and in fact the subcommittee is in possession of a letter written by Judge Simpson which reads as follows:

GENERAL AMERICAN OIL CO. OF TEXAS,
Dallas, Texas, March 29, 1949.

Lt. Col. BURTON F. ELLIS,
Assistant Army Judge Advocate,
Headquarters Sixth Army, Presidio of San Francisco, Calif.

DEAR COLONEL ELLIS: Yours of the 23d instant is acknowledged.

During the progress of this war crimes investigation it was not practicable for us to have the benefit of your views for which I was very sorry. However, we were able to get a right accurate picture of the situation.

I had a great deal of sympathy for Mr. Everett who appeared to me to be prompted only by a desire to represent his clients conscientiously and well. He may have been overzealous but I can forgive this in a lawyer when I think he is sincere. You might be interested to know I had information lately that Colonel Everett had a severe heart attack and is in a serious condition.

Judge Van Roden and I got to be very good friends indeed and I felt greatly disappointed when I read in newspapers and periodicals the very extreme statements he had been making, statements which were based upon allegations rather than proof. He was certainly not being helpful nor constructive in any sense and I repeat that in my opinion he does us all a disservice.

Sincerely yours,

GORDON SIMPSON.

The speeches made by Judge Van Roden were picked up by an organization called the National Council for the Prevention of War. Since that time, which was December 1948, this organization has through every media possible, publicized these charges.[15] This point will be discussed in some detail later. The subcommittee heard both Judge Van Roden and representatives of the National Council for the Prevention of War, and in fact had them on the stand at the same time.[16] The only impression that could be arrived at, after listening to that discussion, was that there was so much conflict between their testimony that the subcommittee believes that it has secured the whole truth from neither of the witnesses.

It is the opinion of the subcommittee that the report of the Simpson Commission, insofar as it pertained to the 12 Malmedy prisoners, was not complete in that no witnesses were heard or evidence received from the prosecution staff or those engaged in pretrial investigations.[17] Since all the facts in the case were not considered before the conclusions

[12] Subcommittee files, Simpson Report; subcommittee hearings, p. 259.
[13] Subcommittee files, Simpson Report; subcommittee hearings, p. 258.
[14] Subcommittee hearings, p. 1092; committee files, Progressive magazine.
[15] Subcommittee confidential files; article from the Progressive.
[16] Subcommittee hearings, p. 1102 et seq.
[17] Subcommittee hearings, p. 258.

were reached, the subcommittee does not see how the conclusions can be sound, especially since the Simpson report states in part:

> The record of trial, however, sufficiently manifests the guilt of the accused to warrant the findings of guilty. We conclude that any injustice done the accused against whom death sentences have been approved will be adequately removed by commutation of the sentences to imprisonment for life. This we recommend.

Insofar as Judge Van Roden's statements are concerned, the subcommittee has sought out the principal source of some of these statements. One of the witnesses, Eble,[18] is a confirmed liar and criminal in whom the subcommittee places no credence whatsoever. Judge Van Roden has shown very poor judgment in publicizing such statements without corroborating the facts. Had the Simpson Commission interviewed Eble, with his record of embezzlement and perjury before them, the subcommittee is certain that they would have decided his testimony could not be believed.

There is no question that the publication of these charges has caused considerable anxiety in the minds of some Americans who may have read them, because they are so completely foreign to the American principles of fair play. Far more serious, however, is the effect that the publication of these articles has had on our occupation forces in Germany.[19] There, they have been accepted because of the cloak of authority given them by Judge Van Roden and various other prominent American officials who have accepted his statements, and the releases of the National Council for the Prevention of War, as fact, and have publicized them through their own efforts.

Concurrently with the study of the Simpson Commission, General Clay referred the Malmedy case to the Administration of Justice Review Board for its consideration.[20] This Board was to study irregularities that arose in legal proceedings within the theater, and it made a careful and analytical study of charges of irregularities in the Malmedy case. It is believed that the facts introduced before this Board, which is hereinafter referred to as the Raymond Board, were much more complete than those considered by the Simpson Commission.

Colonel Raymond, who was the senior member of the Board, testified in detail before the subcommittee.[21] He stated categorically, as did General Hargaugh, another Board member, that in his opinion there had been no physical mistreatment by the American interrogation team for the purpose of securing confessions.[22] Rigorous examination failed to shake him in his position. However they did find other items such as the use of the mock trial, ruses, strategems, etc., had been used.[23] This Board made no recommendations on sentences.

The subcommittee takes note of the fact that in addition to all of these reviews and investigation, General Clay himself instituted a study of and personally studied and passed upon the 12 death sentences in the Malmedy case.[24] This in effect was another review of these 12 cases. As a result of this subsequent review by General Clay, 6 of the 12 were commuted to life imprisonment, and 6 of the death sentences were reconfirmed.[24] No death sentence was confirmed if it

---

[18] Subcommittee hearings, p. 1513 et seq.
[19] Subcommittee confidential files.
[20] Subcommittee hearings, p. 72.
[21] Subcommittee hearings, pp. 72 et seq.
[22] Subcommittee hearings, pp. 87 et seq., 1148.
[23] Subcommittee hearings, appendix; also files, Raymond report.
[24] Subcommittee hearings, p. 1160.

resulted from or was supported by evidence obtained through the use of mock trials, or if it was based solely on the extrajudicial statements made by other defendants in the Malmedy case, which later were repudiated.[25] Even in the six cases where the sentences were commuted, General Clay stated that he was certain of the guilt of the prisoners, but would not approve the death penalty unless the record was perfectly clear. A typical statement on this point is quoted from the case of Friedrich Christ. General Clay states in pertinent part as follows:

> To my mind, Christ was a principal in these murders. I believe as does the judge advocate that he was a leading participant. Circumstantially, there can be no doubt but that he was present and, as an officer, took no action to prevent the crime. Knowing this, it is difficult not to approve the death penalty for this cold-blooded killer. However, to do so would be to accept the evidence which may have resulted only from the improper administration of justice. Excluding this evidence in its entirety in as far as direct participation of Christ is concerned, there is no doubt that he was present, and circumstantially did nothing to prevent these murders. Thus, I have no hesitancy in approving a life sentence. It is with reluctance but with the firm air of fairly administered justice that I commute the death sentence to life imprisonment.

The subcommittee is impressed by the thoroughness of General Clay's final review. As pointed out earlier, it believes that the use of the mock trials so prejudiced the thinking of all who reviewed this case that they resulted in otherwise guilty men escaping the death sentence or perhaps going entirely free. It is the considered opinion of the subcommittee that the Army in reaching its final conclusion in these cases ruled out any evidence secured by improper procedures during the pretrial interrogation, or as a result of procedural errors made by the court.

Personnel

One of the matters which has disturbed the subcommittee considerably is the type of personnel which has frequently been employed on both investigative and legal phases of the war crimes program. It is recognized that after the end of the war almost everyone with sufficient points made a determined effort to get back home.[26] This left the military establishment in Europe in a precarious position insofar as trained personnel for carrying on its military government activities was concerned. It was essential that German speaking personnel be available, and it is perfectly natural that many who had command of the German language were called into investigative and legal work.

First of all, the subcommittee feels that the war crimes cases would have been much better handled had the pretrial investigation been conducted by trained investigators with sufficient knowledge of the law to permit a development of the case along legal lines. It was found that many of the persons engaged in this work had had no prior criminal investigative experience whatsoever, and had been former grocery clerks, salesmen, or engaged in other unrelated trades or professions.[27] It was also found that a surprisingly high percentage of these persons were recently naturalized American citizens.[28]

[25] Subcommittee hearings, appendix; Clay's releases on 12 death cases.
[26] Subcommittee hearings, pp. 200, 1054.
[27] Analysis of background of personnel engaged in investigational work. Individual testimony of witnesses.
[28] Analysis of record, see individual's statements on this point.

This subcommittee wants to make it clear that it is not condemning the efforts or the loyalty of any group of persons or individuals, but it does feel that it was unfortunate that more native-born, trained American citizens were not available to carry out this most important function. The natural resentment that exists within a conquered nation was aggravated by the fact that so many of the persons handling these matters were former citizens of that country.

With few exceptions the experience of the lawyers in the practice of criminal cases both for the prosecution and for the defense appears to have been of only average caliber.[29] Schools were started to overcome some of the lack of trial experience on the part of many of the lawyers.[30] In matters of such a serious nature as war crimes, the minimum requirements for lawyers for this branch of service should be well above average. Again the subcommittee does not wish to appear to be criticizing the efforts or the results of the individuals concerned, but in pointing toward the future, it recommends strongly that adequate planning be initiated to make certain that trained personnel will be available to carry out these duties in event of another war. Particularly it is felt that a well-established and well-organized reserve program, with commitments made in advance for service beyond the end of hostilities, should be immediately inaugurated and carried forward progressively through the years of peace.

III

MOTIVATION BEHIND THE CURRENT AGITATION CONCERNING WAR CRIMES IN GENERAL AND THE MALMEDY CASE IN PARTICULAR

During the early stages of its inquiry into this matter, the subcommittee became conscious of the unusual activity in this case of certain organizations and individuals. Admittedly the charges that had been made were serious in character and, if true, would convict American military personnel of grave errors of judgment and operation. However, due to the manner in which the allegations in this case were being handled, it was also clear that no matter what the facts were in the case, in the minds of a great many Americans and practically all Germans, the allegations were accepted as fact. This was certain to damage the American position in Germany.

The subcommittee fully understands that one of the underlying forces in this connection is found in the vigorous efforts of defense counsel to improve the position of their clients through every means possible. If this were the only factor there would be little cause for comment from the subcommittee, particularly since the affidavits of the accused, in part, have been capable of being checked by the subcommittee.

Representative leaders of both the Catholic and Protestant faiths in Germany, particularly those in Bavaria and around Stuttgart, have been interested in the trials of war criminals. The subcommittee endeavored to find and evaluate the reasons therefor. It appears to your subcommittee that the members of the clergy have been motivated by a sincere Christian endeavor to assist their parishioners during a time of uncertainty and trouble. Such interest is entirely understandable and the subcommittee can see no reason for criticism

---

[29] Subcommittee hearings, pp. 427, 1356.
[30] Subcommittee hearings, p. 1390.

of the clergy.   It should be noted that their activities are not confined to the Malmedy case alone, but have been aimed at the entire scope of war crimes and the administration of prisons throughout Germany where war criminals are confined.   Your subcommittee believes that there is a danger that these sincere Christian efforts of these well-intentioned clergy may be used by others to further causes which are foreign to the fundamental sentiment which motivated the clergy to interest themselves in such cases.

However, other factors were developed during the investigation which, for obvious reasons, cannot be explained in detail in the subcommittee report since it might interfere with the later implementation of the subcommittee recommendations.   Through competent testimony submitted to the subcommittee, it appeared that there are strong reasons to believe that groups within Germany are taking advantage of the understandable efforts of the church and the defense attorneys as well as in other ways to discredit the American occupation forces in general.[31]   One ready avenue of approach has been through the attacks on the war-crimes trials in general and the Malmedy case in particular.   The subcommittee is convinced that there is an organized effort being made to revive the nationalistic spirit in Germany through every means possible.   There is evidence that at least a part of this effort is attempting to establish a close liaison with Communist Russia.   These matters, of course, must be judged against the back drop of the current situation in Europe and their probable effect in the event of a war involving Russia and the United States.   Everything done to weaken the prestige of the United States and our occupation policies will play an important part in any emergency.

Many of the convicted in the various war-crimes trials are former prominent Nazis, both civilian and military.   In the Malmedy case alone there are three German generals, one an outstanding SS general, as well as officers of lesser rank who were excellent combat leaders.[32]   The desire of their former compatriots to have such persons released is undoubted.   The implications are so serious that they cannot be disregarded by our country.   In the event of the withdrawal of the American occupation forces, it is quite probable that there would be efforts made to have a general amnesty program to release these former Nazis and SS officers.   That in itself is a most important consideration; but, in the event there is a larger plan to associate such individuals with the Communist forces of Europe, the problem is greatly aggravated,   The subcommittee believes that such a situation presents dangerous possibilities.   Whether the organization has proceeded beyond the wishful-thinking stage and is making headway is a matter for further study and investigation,

It is significant that many of the figures involved in this situation are in constant communication with individuals, and organizations in the United States.   In particular, one individual, who testified before the subcommittee, and who is reported to be a keyman in this situation, stated that he had been in regular and frequent communication with the National Council for the Prevention of War in the United States.[33]   This was deemed to be extremely significant because before going to Germany the subcommittee had noted that most of the extraordinary

---

[31] Subcommittee confidential files.
[32] Record of trial.
[33] Subcommittee hearings, p. 1160 et seq.

claims being made in this case, and the systematic publication of material concerning it, was through this organization. Representatives of the organization testifying before the subcommittee confirmed this belief by admissions on the witness stand.

The subcommittee, through outside investigation, has determined that the National Council for the Prevention of War and other organizations have maintained a constant correspondence with certain people in Germany and other persons interested in this case. Through these efforts, most of the allegations made in this case have become accepted as fact, and our prestige in Germany thereby adversely affected. The subcommittee is aware of the fact that the National Council for the Prevention of War is not on any of the so-called subversive lists that are maintained, but that it has been considered as an extreme pacifist organization for some time. Notwithstanding the subcommittee is convinced that its activities in this matter, which go far beyond the Malmedy case, have been most damaging to the national interests of our country, and to the cause of peace. The subcommittee feels strongly that the proper investigations should be made to determine the real motivation in back of the activities of this organization and the influence it has had on many individuals within the United States who have accepted as fact the allegations publicized by it. Other organizations which have been similarly interested should also be studied. Since adequate investigational facilities are not available to the Congress, it is believed that the proper agencies of the Government should pursue this matter until all the facts have been developed, and that such action should be taken as the facts would seem to warrant.

The subcommittee recommends that—

1. The Secretary of Defense, through proper channels, request the United Nations to thoroughly study the problem of war crimes; that uniform rules of procedure be agreed upon for the trial of war criminals, as distinct from prisoners of war, and, as rapidly as possible, that such rules be made a part of the codes of justice of the various nations. It is believed that such rules should provide more civilian participation in war-crimes cases than present procedures allow. Pending decision on this matter by the international agencies, necessary legislation should be introduced to remove any legal obstacles in the way of remedial procedural action by the United States.

2. The State Department and the Department of Defense employ no civilians on military-government work who have not been American citizens for at least 10 years. Provisions should be made to waive such requirements in individual and specific cases except for positions involving important questions of administrative or judicial policy.

3. Military personnel engaged in war-crimes work should meet the same citizenship requirements.

4. The Department of Defense should institute a reserve program leading to the creation of a pool of trained investigators and lawyers for war-crimes work who would be committed to serve beyond the cessation of hostilities. Since legislation on this point is required, it should be submitted promptly for the consideration of the Congress. Only through the availability of such trained personnel can procedural mistakes and mistakes of judgment be avoided.

5. The Department of Defense or other appropriate agencies should carefully investigate the possibility of the existence of a plan to revive the German nationalistic spirit by discrediting the American military government.   It should also determine if this is a part of a larger plan to bring parts of Germany into closer relationship with the Soviet Union.

6. The Department of Justice should determine whether or not activities are being carried on in this country which are of such a nature as to discredit and injure American prestige and our public interest in Germany.   If such should be established, appropriate action should be taken under proper Federal statutes.   If additional legislation is required, appropriate recommendations should be made to the Congress.

O

www.ingramcontent.com/pod-product-compliance
Lightning Source LLC
Chambersburg PA
CBHW081541280526
45788CB00010B/3313